NORMAN

BY GARETH

A laugh, a smile, a song, appendicitus. Norman Pace – proud possessor of the boyish face, perennial proponent of fun, mirth and the rhythm method.

Norman grew up as a boy in Newark, later he grew up as a girl in Middlesex. I don't know why fate should throw us together, I don't know why we should hit it off so well, and I don't know why it takes the Earth a year to revolve around the sun; but I know this – a drink's too wet without one.

The first time I met Norman we had just been reincarnated. It was in Mrs Palm's Sauna and Massage Parlour, as I recall. I can't remember what either of us had come back as, but I knew there was an electricity between us.

We met later, in our present form. He was in a play somewhere off Shaftesbury Avenue – Somewhere off Shaftesbury Avenue always struck me as a particularly original title for a play. Norman's talents shone through, he had a special gift which I was very jealous of, it was an electric radio alarm. We teamed up, but Hale and the Electric Radio Alarm didn't seem to get much work, so Hale and Pace were born. How I remember those early days with Norm. Those times he'd laugh, he'd dance, he'd cry, he'd sing, he'd recite poetry, but I suppose Indian food affects different people in different ways.

At one historic performance Norman decided to bare his soul, we were promptly banned from the theatre and he was lucky not be arrested. Norman has a unique relationship with his audience, he has always had the ability to touch his followers, which requires an extremely flexible back.

A romancer – yes indeed. Many a heart has he stolen, which explains why he no longer works part-time at Papworth Hospital.

Unbelievably, Norman can become depressed at times. He won't want you to know this, but yes, behind that clown's make-up we find some of his wife's make-up. The tears of a clown, the mascara of a missus. Like so many comedians before him we see, on the outside, a happy-go-lucky everyday kind of guy, but underneath there lurks a happy-go-lucky everyday kind of guy.

I think we can all learn something from that! ▪

HOW TO BE A RON

Learn how to become a 'Ron' and your troubles are over. This once in a lifetime offer will show you how to

★ BULLY YOUR FRIENDS AT SCHOOL

★ EXTORT MONEY FROM SMALL BUSINESSMEN

★ USE A CHAINSAW FOR CIRCUMCISION

★ DOPE RACEHORSES

★ BE PHOTOGRAPHED WITH SHOWBIZ CELEBRITIES

★ BE A PERSONAL FRIEND OF A RUBBERCLAD JUSTICE OF THE PEACE

★ HAVE A BUDGIE CALLED JOEY

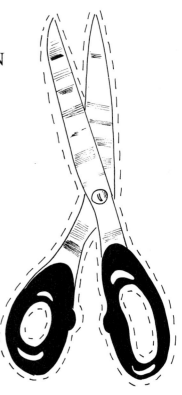

Yes, you can MANAGE your troubles away and all you have to do is send RON and RON the entire contents of your bank account, building society accounts and piggybank.

Just make your last will and testament over to RON and RON today and stick it in the post, or RON will stick the post in you. Send to:

RON and RON Co.
c/o Central Bank
Zurich
or
SWEATY SUZIE'S SAUNA
AND MASSAGE,
London, E.14.

This book belongs to:

~~genghis khan~~

~~adolf hitler~~

adolf
4
Poland
(true)

ACKNOWLEDGEMENTS

We would like to thank those people who have beavered
behind the scenes: Steve Lockett who has provided the illustrations,
Anthony Grant for the photographs, Linda Wade for her
imaginative design, and Nêst Elena Phillips for her artwork.

Gareth Hale and Norman Pace

THE HALE & PACE
BOOK OF
WRITES & RONS

Arrow Books

Jacket and text designed by Linda Wade
Cartoons and illustrations by Steve Lockett
Photographs and Dali illustration by Anthony Grant

Arrow Books Limited
62-65 Chandos Place, London WC2N 4NW

An imprint of Century Hutchinson Limited

London Melbourne Sydney Auckland
Johannesburg and agencies throughout
the world

First published in 1988 by Robson Books Ltd

Arrow edition 1989

© 1988 Gareth Hale and Norman Pace

Printed and bound in Great Britain by
Scotprint, Musselburgh, Scotland

ISBN 0 09 967750 4

When we first read this book, I asked Ron "What do you think of it?" and Ron said "It's a load of steaming crap". Then I remembered that Ron can't read, so I read it to him at bedtime and he still said "It's a load of steaming crap", which is the highest compliment Ron could possibly pay anything.

We agreed to write this foreword for Hale and Pace because they're witty, talented and they let us give their wives one . . . as long as they can watch. They're good lads and they cough up regularly, especially if you puncture their lungs. These boys are talented writers. They use joined-up, capital letters, the lot; and to save making any mistakes they always keep a rubber handy. Which ain't such a bad idea these days.

So what is this book all about then, I hear you silently ask? To you, it's about having a laugh. To us, it's about making lots of money 'cos we get half the Royalties which is equivalent to the Queen Mum's legs. Ron ain't interested in humour. He had his humour surgically removed and sold it to a Greek restaurant owner who serves it up a quid at a time with a portion of pitta bread. How Pitta got in the bread is another story.

But I'm divergin' although Ron ain't 'cos he lost his cherry when he was sixteen. We have a simple message for you readers. BUY THIS BOOK. If you've already bought it, you're safe. But if you're one of those tight bastards in W.H. Smiths standing at the shelves having a crafty read for free, remember, your fingerprints are on the cover, and if you don't buy this book now, me and Ron are gonna shoot up your gaff, if your missus is called Gaff that is. And, what's more, Ron here might have to stick his hand down your throat, pull out your bladder and wear it as a swimming hat. 'Nuff said.

GARETH

BY NORMAN

What's in a name? Well it's an anagram of mane, if you know what I mean, which is another anagram of name. Mean, I mean. So what's in the name Gareth? Well, it's almost a palindrome of The Rag, but more importantly, if you take the G off, then you'll have nothing covering your naughty bits, and also it sounds like someone with a lisp saying "Arse", which brings me on to the man himself.

I think that the first thing that appealed to me about Gareth was his splendid facial hair. I knew, when I met him, in 1971, that anyone with the ability to grow whiskers with such arrogant ease was a man not to be trifled with, or any other kind of pudding for that matter. As I recall, at that time, Gareth had managed to grow the Post-Pubescent Ring, which unlike most eighteen year olds, he didn't keep in his trousers, but underneath his chin. If you think of an underfertilised version of Manfred Mann's beard then you're not a mile away from it. Unless you live at the other end of the Mile End Road.

Over the years, this ability to grow hair has followed Gareth all over his face. Until, in 1987, it finally came to rest, like a dormant caterpillar, upon his top lip, where it has lived quietly ever since with nought but the occasional bogey and some half-digested Chicken Madras for company.

People often ask me, and I usually say yes. They also often ask me, "What is the secret of Gareth's comedy genius? Surely," they say, "it can't just be the moustache?" Well, no. Although Gareth's moustache is one of the funniest in the business (rivalling even that of Fatima Whitbread), let's face it, Man Doth Not Laugh By Hair Alone. Choke, yes, but laugh . . . no way hose . . . as they say in the stocking business. So, you ask, what is it, apart from the 'tache, that makes Gareth so screamingly hilarious? Let me tell you, and this word needs a paragraph to itself.

Lager.

Although both are potent forces in their own right, the 'tache and the lager when kept apart are comically containable. But when welded together across the rim of a pint glass, you'd better stick your sense of humour in the stirrups for a joke is about to be born.

That's Gareth in a nutshell, or a pint pot. He's a nice bloke, but a word of warning. If by some quirk of fate you are in a pub one evening and you spot a familiar moustache attached to a pint of lager then I'll just say this to you. When you tap him on the shoulder make sure you duck, because the wit is about to hit the fan ■

CUT OUT RON

Cut-out your own Ron
with our giveaway cut-out
paper scissors. Cut-out Ron's
clothes, cut-out Ron's togs and
then cut-out your own liver.

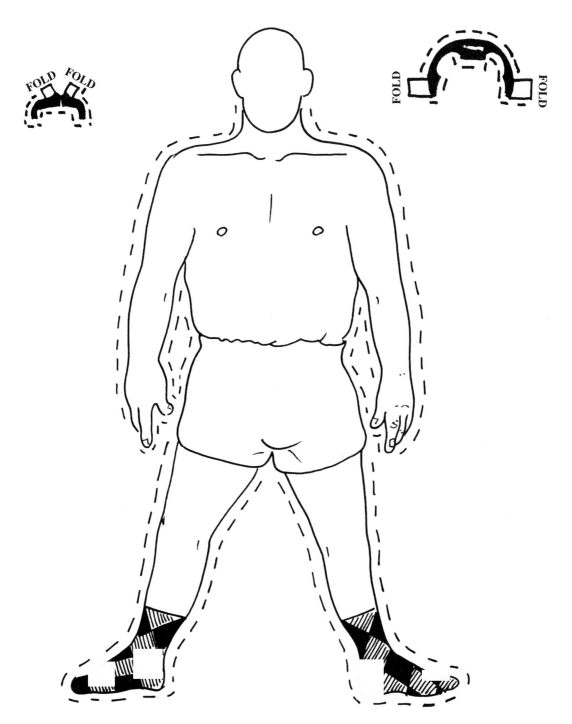

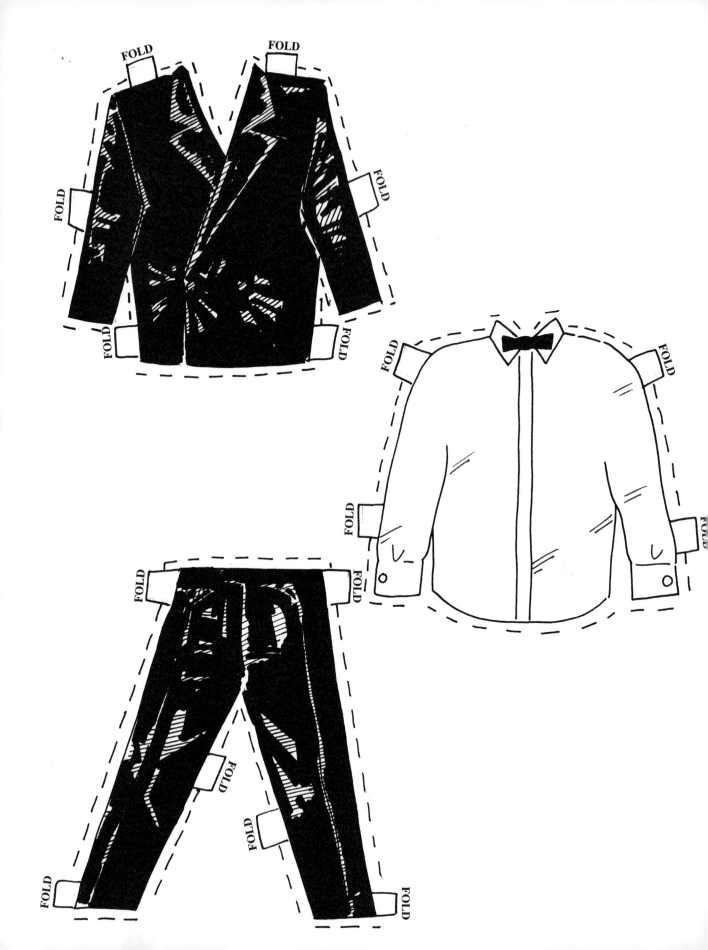

**CUT OUT
AND PLACE
IN WIFE'S MOUTH**

**STOCKING MASK
RON WEARS THIS
DURING SEX**

**RON'S PYJAMA CASE
FOLD AND PLACE
AT END OF BED**

Shakespeare's Alphabet

(William Shakespeare:
a man of letters)

AB or not **AB**
C is **D** question
Whether **E** tis nobler in the mind
To suff-**F**er the **G**'s and **H**'s of outrageous fortune
I to take **J**s against a sea of
troub**L**s and by **O P** posing end them?
To **Q**; to **R**; no more;
and by a **S**leep to say we end
the heartache and thousand natural shocks
that flesh is heir to.
T is a consummation devoutly **U V** wished.
To die, to sleep, to sleep perchance to **W**
My, there's the rub.
For **X** in that sleep of death **Y** dreams may come
zzzzzzzzzzzzzzzzzzzzzzzzzzzzzzz

ARE YOU
looking for a challenging and rewarding career?

DO YOU
want action and adventure?

COULD YOU
survive an enemy missile attack?

COULD YOU
defend yourself against up to thirty opponents in unarmed combat?

COULD YOU
hold your nerve in the face of a riot?

If yes then YOU'RE the type of man we're looking for.

TURN OVER

JOIN THE
PROFESSIONALS
BE A TEACHER

MEMORIES OF INDIA

Ode to a Load

A poem by Sir John Betterman
Thunlam Gungadin

How blessed are we that can taste
That fragrant finest food
In restaurants and take aways
Meat dansak, vindaloo.

That fiery food both spiced and full
That floods the gut and burns
Both savoury and delicate
That maketh tastebuds yearn.

An hour or two after vindaloo
I can hear intestines gargle
And when they stop I oft will drop
A highly perfumed fardle.

The rumbling knell doth anger well
And I must move straightway
To seat myself upon that throne
And do without delay.

The trousers first and then the pants
And thrust towards the floor
And to save embarrassment
Make sure you've locked the door.

And now at last an opening blast
That shakes the bathroom suite
It thunders through the silent air
Rattling the toilet seat.

A newspaper or paperback
Will help to pass the hours
Sit back and enjoy the weather
You're in for thundery showers.

A sigh, a heave, a grunt, a groan
Brings monster from his cave
The serpent slowly slips away
Into a watery grave.

And if I live till eighty,
Then I will tell my son
Never leave that sacred chamber
Until the job is done.

H & P'S HIGH FAT DIET

BEFORE

AFTER

Ten years ago, Gareth and Norman were both fit and trim teachers of Physical Education, but after only TEN years on the H & P High Fat Diet they have turned themselves into the quivering masses of blubber that they are today.

GARETH SAYS: 'Yeah, it was pretty tough going especially in the early stages, but the effort was worth it. The High Fat Diet is what gave me the confidence to become a comedian. It's difficult to be funny when you're too thin. Ask Jasper Carrot.'

NORMAN SAYS: 'I took the diet too seriously at first. In fact I used to suffer from Fatorexia Nervosa, and often I would secretly run out of the toilet and force myself not to be sick after a bucket of curry. The High Fat Diet, though, changed my life and it also doubled my time for the 100 metres.'

Other funny people whose lives have changed because of the diet:

CHRIS BIGGINS 'I owe it all to the diet'

BERNARD MANNING 'I've been on it since birth'

SID LITTLE 'It was the diet that made Eddie funny'

NIGEL LAWSON 'The diet improved my stand-up act no end'

THE DIET

Wake up in the morning. Eat as much as you can all day long and drink a lot of alcohol. Do this every single day of your life especially when you are ill and don't feel like it. These are the tough times but stick at it and you can have a figure like this:

EXERCISES

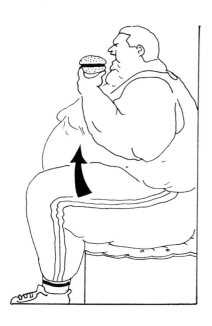

Hamburger Lifting
Sit in chair. Lift Hamburger to mouth. Repeat 20 times per day.

Jogging for Men
Strip to the waist. Take a firm grip of your flabby breasts and jog them up and down a bit. This will not get you fit but it may arouse you sufficiently so that you can find out where your penis disappeared to.

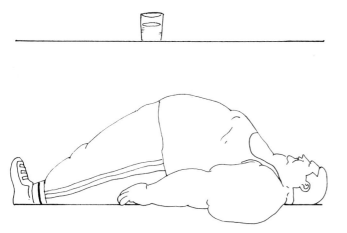

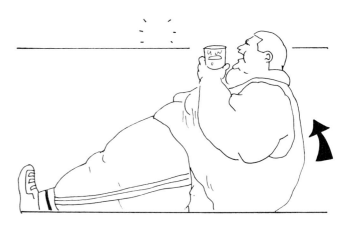

Lager Sit-Ups
Sit up and drink a lot of lager.

Sauna
Yes. If you can get through the door.

Running
Don't do it.

Rowing
Have as many rows as you like, especially with the wife after a good session of Lager Sit-Ups.

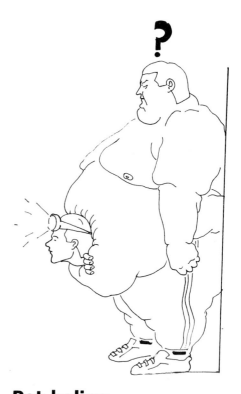

Pot-holing
Be careful of people who want to do this in your navel.

AH CONDOM
FOR SAFER SMOKING

DRINKS WORDY

GARETH
Angus McBeerbely. Do ye no think there's a nip in the air tonight? It's no mild out, it's bitter.

NORMAN
Truman, truman. It's a wee bit chilly around the old orangeboom.

GARETH
How's Barbie?

NORMAN
Since she's been off the bottle, no one can wine like Barbican.

GARETH
Och — she's alcohol free?

NORMAN
Aye — before she'd never say Malibu to a goose but now her behaviour's really Grolsch. It must be the creme of the menthe. Are you still working at the distillery still?

GARETH
Watney?

NORMAN
Are you still working at the distillery still?

GARETH
Per-no-d — no-d — no-d. I wondered what you ferment for a moment. They gave me the dry sack.

NORMAN
You've had your last orders then.

GARETH
Don't get saki with me pal.

NORMAN
Sorry. That must have stirred you up a bit eh?

GARETH
No, I was shaken, not stirred. I was caught in the cellar noggin with this Dubonny wee lassie.

NORMAN
Was it Sherry? Rosee? It must have been Cherry then.

GARETH
No, you know Cherry's always on top. It was Martini.

NORMAN
Oh no.

GARETH
And you know what Martini's like.

NORMAN
Aye, I do. Any time, any place, anywhere, it's bottoms up and down in one.

GARETH
But I didnae chaser, Bianco's my girlfriend. Let's face it, Martini doesnae campari wi' Bianco. She's not even one sixth of the gill. Well I was just about to reach parts others cannae reach when the Boss came in and said 'Time, gentlemen please'.

NORMAN
Bloody Mary, explaining that must have been a drop of the hard stuff.

GARETH
Well I told him she was trying to drink me under the table, but she collapsed. All I was trying to do was give her the kirsch of life, you know, breathalyser.

NORMAN
What do you mean?

GARETH
Blow into the bag.

NORMAN
Did he believe you?

GARETH
He told me to Smirnoff. The Bar Steward.

NORMAN
You mean you didn't have a quick one for the road, a skinfull.

GARETH
Mind your own Buck's Fizzness.

DRINKS WORDY

DALI ON GOLF

What enormity of surprise for me when Mysterallis rang me up. As I held the lobster to my ear I could hardly believe my oceans of good luck. For many years have I loved Mysterallis, his fanaticism, his strong rebellious heart, his sand-iron technique, but most, his mackerel flavoured trousers. Of course, of course, of course, of course, of course, of course, of course I would love to play in the Pro-Surrealist Golf Championship. So I refused.

But then I changed my dmni, and then I changed my mind.

We started the match at 7.00 in the year 2000 Grecian time, the sun burst through the skies like a tuna in a casserole. I carried over my shoulder what Mysterallis called a golf bag. It was like a huge empty phallus filled with pieces of stick that had an iron or a wooden foot. The sticks of wood that had a wooden foot wore a condom, and were numbered 1–4.

Mysterallis put a perfectly white sphere on the ground and hit it in the direction of a flag many anaconda-lengths away. It landed near a pile of greyhound's vomit that was being raped by a three-legged rhinocerous.

It was my turn to play. I struck the white sphere with the wooden-footed stick, Mysterallis called it a driver. It reminded me of one in New York who had driven me from the airport. We got nearer to what was called a green, it was flat like an enormous chessboard, a chessboard that was painted with emeralds. In the middle of this green green was a pole that indicated where the White Rabbit had taken Alice.

We had to chase the white spheres, our White Rabbits, into the hole so that they would not be late. For this I used a special stick, it was made entirely of butter. I only hit mine once and it disappeared. Mysterallis obviously loves me deeply because he said I have golden bollocks.

We walked on a strangely mysterious journey, trying many times to make our White Rabbit disappear. The victor would be the man who smacked the rabbit's bottom the least amount of times. Mysterallis talked to me of my paintings, my extraordinary genius, and the fluidity of my strokes. He also talked much of the colour green, he was a nose-fetishist who spent most of the afternoon picking up bogies. He philosophically discussed crime and punishment, he believed in going down the fair way. He had an aversion for strumpets, harlots and whores, for many times he warned me about the danger of losing your balls in the rough.

It was a day of much learning for me despite my limitless capabilities. As we sat in the Nigh Teethole, we exchanged stories. He, of how he drove the green at the Belfry, me, of my venture to manufacture jockstraps for herniated giraffes. As the lush, lubricating liqueurs washed over our palates he seemed to understand more about why the White Rabbit should not be late.

Swedish Romance

A NEW SHORT STORY BY

MILLICENT TULLE

Finga Johansen contemplated what a beautiful evening it had been. She loved the wine, the excitement, the atmosphere of the place; but most of all she loved Lars Helstrom, that handsome hunk of hardness. She thought about her jealous friends, how they envied her lovely Lars; maybe one day they might be lucky. He had returned, there was a slow burning smile etched upon his finely featured face.

Outside he athletically slid into her Volvo, as she pressed the starter button. The engine throbbed readily. It was not long before they reached his immaculate bachelor penthouse flat. It was not long before they were sipping chilled champagne. It was not long before they were swaying to the insistent rhythms of the music. It was not long, but she didn't mind.

How she would long and pine for moments like these, long and pine – just like a fir tree. The moment was here, Lars stared into her clear welcoming eyes. He got out his geyornansplat and proudly placed it on the table. Finga ran her finger the length and width of the geyornansplat, it was wonderful. Her mungenflop caught his eye, he clutched one to his splitzloben, it was good.

They couldn't stop now. His finger caressed Finga's vangelstrop, steady, determined movements of his pumpgofelt made her catch her breath in tiny pert inhalations. Finga took the initiative and slowly mounted an assault on his stromjensonson, her voomtrombles made him gulp and gasp, again and again. He shrieked as she brought him to a magnificently engineered bunganalafson boliksonberg.

It had been marvellous, but now it was over. It had been a great game of chess, but now it was finished. So they went into the bedroom and had a bloody good bunk up.

FOOT FETISHISTS CALENDAR

Miss January

SCRATCH 'N' SNIFF

Get some of this . . . Miss January a real triple-decker . . . the scent of
pop-sock, a savour of blackened toenail, topped off with a soupçon of eau de
council house . . . smell these babies and in our mind's eye . . . you'll be
wearing them with no stockings, strolling through the snow in January to buy
twenty No6 from the newsagents. Miss bliss.

C. ONHAM & SONS

CENTRAL LONDON

MAYFAIR
Early Georgian WINDOW. Panoramic view of London, 6″ x 24″ garden. Beautifully kept. Double glazed, very clean. Running water when it's raining. Convenient for shops and transport if you carry it with you. Ideal for 1st time buyer – owner willing to sell open or closed. A snip at £97,995.

KENSINGTON
One bedroom flat, many original features, sliding door entrance. Within striking distance of West End. £450,000. No offers.

WHITEHALL: Friend or Foe Cottage
Detached residence. This compact apartment with attractive gabled roof and open-plan doorway is desirable for anyone 8 feet tall or wearing a ridiculous furry hat. Good view of Changing The Guard. £150,000.

WATERLOO
Cosily sited under the Embankment, with good view of The River, this cardboard box, built to Barratts' highest specifications is a must for all first time visitors to London. Late-drinkers only need apply.

The Ballad of Jockinvar

Gather round and I'll tell you a story
Of a castle that fills men with fear
It might make you feel a bit queasy
Or it might make you feel a bit queer.

G

The castle stood high in Kirk Douglas
A wee little town, och it's true
It was haunted by nosey young pixies
And a slimey green bogey man too.

G

But deep in the bowels of the castle
Lived the most evil thing that could be
It struck fear in the hearts of the mighty
The Ghoulie of Kirk Douglas was he.

G

He was big and nasty and hairy
And the veins bulged out right off his face
His skin was all warty and wrinkly
But with Ghoulies that's often the case.

G

His shoe was the size of a lifeboat
Not to mention the width of his toes
And if ye could get no bed and breakfast
You could kip for the night up his nose.

G

The Ballad of Jockinvar

The Ghoulie dined chiefly on women
He gobbled them up in one go
His taste was for pretty young women
So he'd no survive long in Glasgow.

G

One day he kidnapped a young lassie,
Called Kirsty McDonald McBlack
She was large and tasty and saucy
So everyone called her Big Mac.

G

Now Kirsty she had a fine boyfriend
And young Jockinvar was his name
He was noted for tossing the caber
But he went with the girls just the same.

G

Now when young Jock he found that the monster
Had stolen his Kirsty away,
Wi' his bagpipes he shot up Kirk Douglas
Confronting the monster straightway.

G

The monster he grabbed our young hero
And Jock screamed out loud with surprise
But when you're dragged off by the Ghoulie
It's bound to bring tears to your eyes.

The monster he wickedly crushed Jock
And as Jock's life was ebbing away
He reached for his trusty wee bagpipes
And mournfully started to play.

The Ghoulie's one eye started rolling
And a strange grin spread over his face
With a tip tappy toe he was dancing
Like a loony all over the place.

The monster danced high on the turrets
Hypnotised by the piper's strange sound
Which was played in the key A flat monster
As the Ghoulie fell splat to the ground.

So since that great day in Kirk Douglas
Our lassies are safe from mishap
Coz they know that all hairy great ghoulies
Will always fall into Jock's trap.

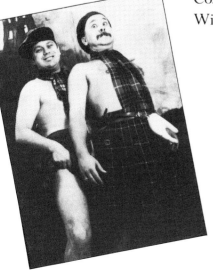

FOR SALE

£25 and under

Five £5 notes
will accept £25.00 o.n.o.

24 One pound coins
bargain at only £24.00
per set. Available at
any bank.

49 50p pieces
for only £24.50p.
Ring your local bank.

MANSION
16 bedrooms, 5 recep.,
3 bathrooms. In 3 acres
of own grounds including
deer park. In residential
part of DONCASTER.
£21.39p o.n.o.

COLOSTOMY BAG
One careful owner. Good
runner. £6 (o.n.o. I've
done it again)

STRAIGHT
BOOMERANGS
£10 for job lot. No
returns.

GLOVES beautiful
kid gloves £10. Genuine
reason for sale – caught
shoplifting in Saudi Arabia.

GOLDEN
BLOWOFFS
contact MIDAS exhausts.

RUSSIAN
ROULETTE GAME
Keep your kids quiet for
hours. Send £20.00 and
s.a.e. to Robert De Niro,
P.O. Box 25, PhnomPhen.

EXPENSIVE
CLOTHES HANGER
Required to marry
Prince Edward.

my name is Barry Bigot and I am a jern jurn Jerne a reporter for a newspaper called the Scum. It is a good newspaper and I like righting for it. when I grow up I would like to write for the BEano which is the best I think. I am BritiSH and I live in BRItain and I like being British because it is good. AND mrs FAtcha is British and I like her and I love her and I would like to marry her if she had bigger tits!

the onion joke

Barry 4 :-) maggie

Some people are british, who I do not think should be British and should be sent back to wear they come from unless they have got big tits!!

dad mum adolph I think the common market is stupid and I think we should get out of it in case we catch dids! my friend Genghis says that his dad knows a man wiv aids and thats cos he is a Poof!, the man not his dad. I think that only old people should have aids cos old people are def and aidsu will help them hear better and I think it is not fairy that all poofs have dids cos it means that old people can't have any. I think Poofs should be sent bank to where they come from unless they have got big tits! ←a poof!

written by Barry Bigot   age 42

ANATOMY OF A WALLY

"Come to bed" lazy eye ▷

Hole for "Lager Top" Drinking ◁

Furry Hood for soaking up dribble ◁

Forefinger for holdi up to a friend an shouting "Swi

Chins ▷

For counting up to "Two" ▽ ▽

Flyhole ◁

Other lover ◁

Designer Rip ◁

Anorak – can be worn as a skirt ◁

1st L ◁

GROIN – very small and never used ◁

Brain ▷

Testicle Repository ◁

Pubic Hair ▷

▽ Nappy

Carpet slippers ◁ ▷

Corrugated D Shit Holders ◁

SEXY

INTELLIGENT

LOVING

THOUGHTFUL

HAPPY

SAD

FOOT FETISHISTS CALENDAR

Miss March

SCRATCH 'N' SNIFF

Bring a whiff of the Follies Bergères into your nostrils . . . The sweet aroma of Fanny by Gaslight. Miss March will do exactly that . . . all over your oléfactory organs . . . she can can and she will will. Two Shoes Lautrec was no fool. He had his legs chopped off to get a better sniff of these babies!

The Dead Sea Scrotes

.. And it came to pass that the people called the Disraelis were ruled over by the mighty ledder of all Egypt, the Fairy. None dare offend the Fairy lest he pour his broth upon them for he did rule with an iron fish.

But amongst the men of the Disraelis one stood out and he was known as Noses. And they did pick Noses as their ledder saying he will deliver us, let us follow our Noses.

And he did kneel, and prey saying to the Lord, "who shall reledse the Isrdelites?"

And the Lord did answer saying, "Desmond Dekker shall reledse the Isrdelites."

And Noses did ledd the Disraelis as the Lord made a path through the Red Sea, and they were nearly deafened as the waters ...

... parted. It was then that Noses did run to Mount Sinus, and there did he receive the Ten Commandos.

from the Gospel according to...
...... St. Dislexid.

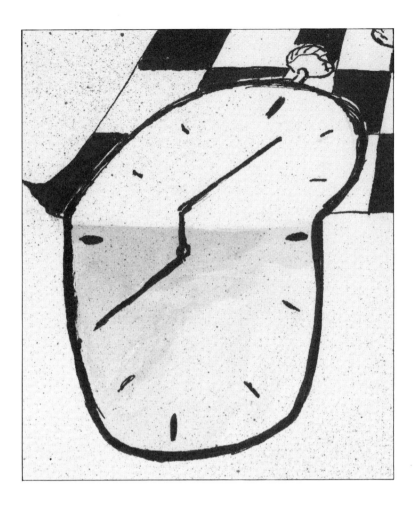

by
CHRISTIAN
DELACROIX-TIDY

Just who does this man think he is fooling! The works of Monsieur Jacques Blojum are nothing more than infantile scrawl delivered with the panache of an unprogrammed robot. This Belgian buffoon festoons me with streamers of confusion, he has no appreciation of line, style, content, composition or artistic interpretation. I have been an art critic for twenty-five years and, as a wearer of a spotted bow tie, brown corduroy jacket, hush puppies and ridiculous glasses, I must confess this man's work is the greatest affront I have ever suffered in my professional life.

People have been raving about this Multi-coloured Messiah, praising his abilities and outrageously imaginative vision. Art experts have been taken in by his amazingly accurate eye for detail, the subtlety of his brushstrokes, and complex use of colour.

Pish, poppycock and twaddle; let me tell you this man has no talent whatsoever, his efforts are puerile and pathetic and, what is more, he never bloody well puts the top back on the toothpaste tube.

If your son went to
public school and
still can't wipe his
own arse — use

NAMBIES

DISPOSABLE NAPPIES
FOR PRATTS

TO BILL WORDSWORTH

I 'ung about all on me Todd,
Waitin' like a stupid sod
Lookin' at nature and that kind of stuff
Passed the time picking navel fluff.

Then Blimey O'Reilly cop an eyefull of these
A bunch of daffs all flutterin' on the breeze
I thought they was daffs, they was yellow an' 'at,
When a bloke says they was tulips I didn't
half feel a pratt.

THE SMOKE

You breathe it every day — you smoke
It's getting to your lungs — you choke
You can't afford to laugh — you joke
You're like a frog when you die — you croak.

PRIME MINISTER

She's got a big pair of knockers
On her door, on her door
And she likes to have a brush up
On the floor, on the floor.
Her husband he is quiet
As a mouse, as a mouse
And she likes to pass a motion
In the House.

She is Maggie, she is Thatcher
She is proud, she is proud
And when she drops a clanger
It is loud, it is loud.
Her husband likes a whisky
He gets tight, he gets tight
Which explains why he is leaning
To the right, to the right.
Thank you — good night.

THINGS YOU SHOULD <u>NEVER</u> SAY TO YOUR BANK MANAGER

When you have your next meeting with your Bank Manager to discuss your overdraft, here are a few things you should not say to him.

'Why are you such an ugly bastard?'

'I thought only teenagers had acne.'

'Stick a finger up your arse and fish for your money.'

'I've had your wife and she's rubbish.'

'Why are your ears stuck on back to front?'

'How do you spell pus-filled little toad?'

'May I urinate in your pocket?'

'I love you. I want to marry you and live in a semi in Sidcup for the rest of my days with two kids, a dog and a four-berth caravanette.'

'I hear your son steals cars.'

'I met your daughter at the clinic.'

'Don't they make that suit in your size?'

'Are you still a virgin?'

'When did you last see your willy, you fat git?'

FOOT FETISHISTS CALENDAR

Miss April

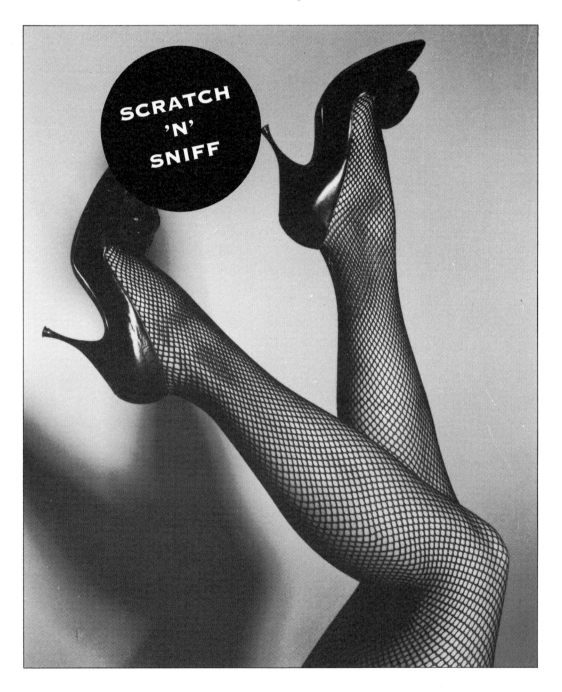

Yummy! Miss April is a must for the first time sniffer. A young, yet bold aroma. Definitely a show with a big nose. A hint of cat's piss, a suggestion of athlete's foot, guaranteed to set the heart and groin pulsing. Miss April, a lady to sniff, to love and to wear with your wife's stockings when you come home from the office.

ROBERT ZIMMERMAN

Ex British Rail
Station Announcer

A quarter to three
Twenty minutes past nine
Half past four
Ten minutes to five
Twenty five to one
Five minutes past eight
Midday midnight afternoon and evening
Seven minutes to eleven
And a quarter to twelve

And the times they are a-changing.

VOTE

FOR THE
BIG FAT NORTHERN
BASTARD PARTY

VOTE FOR ALF SAGGINGBOTHAM
YOUR REPRESENTATIVE
FOR SCROTUM ON TRENT

VOTE FOR ALF SAGGINGBOTHAM

The Man Himself:

Whippet breeder and lover of pigeons, this man is engaged to a ferret. Alf has made great contribution to British industry by developing the foreskin umbrella, when it starts to rain the umbrella grows to twice its normal size. This man is an admirer of t arts, he has his own personal gallery of seaside postcards.

What He Stands For:

1. Unemployment – 'gives you more time in the day to take ferret out to pictures'.

2. The Vote – 'take it away from women, they never bloody use it anyway. Woman's place is chained to mangle not running round country being Prime Minister.'

3. Education – 'Chuff off, no bloody thank you. I had none, and my father before me, and if it's good enough for him, it's good enough for me.'

4. More outside toilets – 'Aye.'

5. Large trousers that come up under your armpits – 'with button fly!'

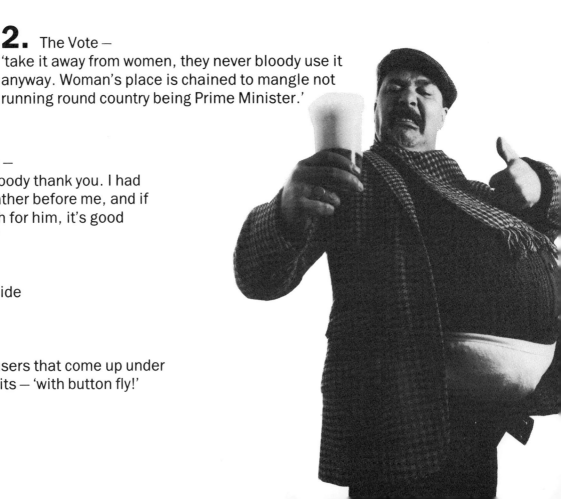

6. Health —
'Compulsory T.B. for all schoolchildren, you have to be cruel to be kind.'

What He Doesn't Stand For:

'I don't stand for,'

1. Nancies

2. Baths not made of tin

3. Colour T.V.s

4. Pint of bitter wi'out 'ead on it.

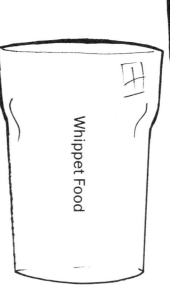

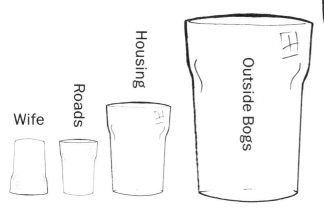

Wife

Roads

Housing

Outside Bogs

Whippet Food

Alf's Pint

VOTE FOR ALF SAGGINBOTHAM.
He Cares About You, He Cares About Me,
but most of all he cares about himself.
YOUR REPRESENTATIVE
FOR SCROTUM ON TRENT

Choosing Your Baby's Name

Anybody who's ever had to choose a baby's name knows how difficult a task it can be. You don't want to choose something too ordinary like the name Gareth or something that makes everybody burst out laughing every time they say it – like the name Norman. You need to find something special, an individual sort of name that is specific to your baby. Here are a few ideas:

* Try giving your baby a name meant for a baby of the opposite sex . . . Archibald for a girl, Wendy if it's a boy. Johnny Cash threatened to do this in his song 'A Boy Named Sue' but I've personally never met a boy who is in fact called Sue so I think Johnny was having us on. Call your son Sue. You may be the first and it's one way of getting your picture in the tabloid newspapers. Think of a really good one and you might make the front page of *The Sun* – Hamster for example. Some other ideas:

Boy's Name	*Girl's Name*
Felicity	**Clint**
Charity	**Rock**
Tamsin	**Arthur**
Racquel	**Lorraine**
Pauline	**Big Tom**

* Foreign names have become very popular in recent years, especially names of Irish, Welsh and Scottish origin. Why not look further afield for your baby's name? In Sweden, for example, the name Bent is very popular for boys, as is Gunnar and Lars. Bjorn is an obvious thought and has the advantage of being easily mispronounced so your son can have the pleasure of saying 'Please Miss, you don't pronounce the "J"' all through his school life.

For the girls Anni-Frid is a must for all ABBA fans. It also has the advantage of having a hyphen in it. However, Scandinavia is not so good for girls' names, although the USA is. The USA has many fine old Red Indian names. Try Minnie-Ha-Ha, a powerful two-hyphen name. Or Mukajawa, which when translated means She-Who-Rides-Many-Moons-Over-Happy-Hunting-Ground-To-Kill-Pony-Soldier. A marvellous name to bore people to death with over the dinner table.

Australia is a happy hunting ground for girls' names. Simply choose a word and put -LENE on the end of it. Hence, Raylene, Charlene, Julene, Marlene and Jolene. With a bit of thought, you can make up your own 'Australian' name for your baby girl. Whatever you choose, it will never be as outrageous as the programme 'Neighbours'. Here are some ideas:

Nipplene	**Bananalene**	**Lenelene**
Diddylene	**Windowlene**	**Ethylene**
Armlene	**Margelene**	**Leapylene**

* Film stars often make up silly names for themselves so that they stand out from the crowd. For example, the name Tuesday Weld. As far as I know, this is the first use of a 'day of the week' as a name since Man Friday, and anyway Friday is not really his first name, because 'Man' is. So why don't you use one of the other six days of the week for your child? If your surname is Knight, for example, choosing the name Saturday for your baby would be quite apt. Some other silly names of film stars:

Meryl Streep
Either name is a good first name

Rip Torn
Named after a particularly difficult birth

Strother Martin
His father got his name the wrong way round on the birth certificate

Hermione Gingold
Of the two I prefer Gingold

Sly Stallone
He certainly is

Dustin Hoffman
Dad couldn't spell Justin

Jodie Foster
Short for Jodhpur

Tyne Daly
Old Geordie newspaper

* You must look to the future. Your baby will still be a child in the year 2001, so maybe you would like to choose a name with modern, even technological, implications. For a girl Polyunsaturate is an interesting thought. Slightly more modern than Marge and if you find it a bit of a mouthful it shortens nicely to Polly. Why stick with just a name? An initial as well as a Christian name can give extra bite. Why call your son Ray when he could be called X-Ray. If you prefer initials instead of a name as many Americans do, why not call your son July August September October November, or JASON for short? You could stick to initials that are of the moment. Why not D.N.A. or R.N.A.? If however you decide to call your son Andrew Ian David Stephen . . . then I would think seriously about using initials. And for parents of more academic bias, even Henry Ignatius Victor could be dangerous.

If you haven't found anything here that suits your taste, do not despair. At least we've got you thinking about it. If you're desperate, then name your baby after somebody you admire. At least that way the world can look forward to a lot of people called Eddie Edwards.

FOOT FETISHISTS CALENDAR

Miss July

SCRATCH 'N' SNIFF

Swing along to the summer sounds and smells of elevated sole music. Thrill to the thought of these babies dancing up and down your back, believe me these odour eaters are good enough to eat. These platforms will take you on an express ride to nirvana. Go on, climb aboard, and breathe in the stench of the wench.

Line up me Lads and Listen well
If you be brave and bold
for I've a tale to tell to you
That'll make your blood run cold
It's a tale of Lust and a tale of death
And a tale of the pirates flag.
So Lend me an ear and Lend me a quid
And throw in a packet of fags me boys
A packet of twenty fags.

47

The Story starts when we set sail
And the seagulls filled the sky
Them seagulls got us all d rage
And they got us in the eye
The bosun worked us night and day
Though a nasty Lisp had he
He said "Sthquare sthaped sthailes on a
                    sthip-sthaped sthip

50

Sthow a sthip sthould be me Lads."
How a Ship-shape ship should be.

No one would say where we were bound
Not one man breathed a breath
But we'd heard that the master of the ship
Was a man called Captain Death
Some say the Captain nearly drowned.
Which drove him off his rocker
Coz he'd sung Last Train To Clarkesville
Down in Davy Jones Locker
Aye in that Little Monkees Locker.

Now no one had seen this Captain Death
Though we'd been eight days at sea
Then we'd heard a shout from down below
And we waited nervously.
The hatch flew back and the sight we saw
Well, it gave each man a shock
For Captain Death stood fierce and bold.
In a bright red sequinned frock me boys
A rather charming sequinned frock.

He held the crew with his one good eye
As he shimmered across the deck
And the wind it played with chiffon scarf
Tied at his manly neck
He said, "Pin back your ears you scum
And I'll tell you why we set sail
For we're bound for Californ-i-a
In search of the great white whale.

For fifteen months we sailed that ship
Through rain and stormy weather
With the Captain steadfast at the wheel
In a jock strap made of leather.
We sighted the whale in the early morn
And chased it through the day
With Captain Death all dressed to kill
In a see-through negligee me boys
The sheerest french negligee.

Well we chased that whale and we killed —
— that whale

An adventure you can't believe
And when we got close up to it
It was enough to make you heave
It was the biggest whale I'd ever seen
All huge and white and blubbery
With skin just like a blow-up doll
You know, all cold and rubbery, boys
All cold and clammy and rubbery.

So thank you all you jolly boys
for the ears that you've been lending
Now the story of the Great White Whale
It has a happy ending.
When we got back to England boys
A celebration they'd been planning
Coz the great white whale what we'd —
— harpooned
Was that bastard Bernard Manning!!

UNDER ABBEY WOOD

–A PLAY FOR VOICES

To begin at the beginning . . .

Abbey Wood, quaint and cute, its stark skyline caught against a darkening backdrop, black stacks of concrete meet the gathering gloom. Night's shadowy cloak shrouds the sleeping minds of those who drift into the welcoming arms of slumber.

Until morning, forgotten are the towerblocks, flats, flatcaps, toecaps, claptrap, cutcrap, fish and chips, lipstick, litter, bitter, pitter-patter, tittle-tattle, nutter, gutter, drunks, punks and puke in the lift.

Only you can hear the addled minds of the addled adolescents, essence of frenzied grope behind bikeshed. Listen as they come to grips with lips and zips.

Dean	Go on Shal
Sharon	Get off!
Dean	Go on Shal
Sharon	Get off, you octopus in teenage-range designer clothing.
Dean	You let Clint do it.
Sharon	Well, Clint's a man of the world, he's got four hairs under each armpit.
Dean	So what, I've got quite an interesting selection of acne, and not just on my face.
Sharon	Well alright, then, but I'll only let you do it if you hum the theme tune to Dynasty while you are doing it.

And so we leave Sharon to fight for her right, and her left.

Now we visit Barry Blubber, British Rail porter, lover of next door's daughter, avid football supporter. Kegbellied, baggy buttocked, the boozy snoozer snoring trumpet – loud, blasts a fruity fanfare from his bugle bum. Lost in a drunken dream he guzzles gobfulls of brain-bending booze.

Barry	Get it down yer son, yeah, I'm twenty two, stone, not years, but I know what's what right, cheers. Get it down yer son, eighteenth pint of lager, and I can still have sex with meself. Come on you reds.

But now for Barry a spring has sprung in his well-sprung bed, and he fights amidst the watery depths with a one-tentacled, unemployed octopus.

Two doors down mortician's assistant, balmy embalmer Sidney Spratt bickers and moans, whines, whinges and complains.

Sidney	Bloody milkman, Express Dairies, trade descriptions, and the binmen, load of bloody rubbish – haha – stop that, almost made meself laugh. Policemen – spotty youths, nurses, supposed to make people get better, walk around in black stockings, shouldn't be allowed. Where's me mates, me muckers, Nobby, Chalky, Ginge, good mates, die for you they would, that's what Ginge did, and the bastard still owed me a fiver. But they're all bastards really. Newsagent – Morning sir – bastard Shop assistant – Can I help you sir, bastard? Bloke at the garage – Lovely day, bastard Illegitimate children – they're alright.

bicker, moan, Whine, Winge, Complain, ETC, ETC,

We must leave them now as sunrise comes, heralding hope for a new day.

Groovy Wordbe

Groovy Wordbender was perhaps the most influential and prolific poet of the 1950s. This messiah of the beat generation urged youngsters to question their lifestyles, their ambitions and the talking clock. His primitively complex rhythm patterns echo the patterns of golfers' trousers the world over. His lust for life and thirst for alcohol made him the leader of a generation. Here is a small selection from his highly acclaimed anthology, 'Hey Baby, my sandal's on fire'.

PLASTIC ■ HIP ■

If chicks give you kicks when you're out on a trip,
— That's hip.
But man it's too drastic to say that's fantastic
— it's plastic.
Don't copy Elvis or you'll bust a pelvis
The pain makes you flip
Uh-oh — plastic hip.

JACK ■ AMNESIAC ■

The rhythm of the congo
Coming from my bongo
Forgotten how the song go
De dum de dum de dodo.

LAUNDERETTE ■

So I smoke a cigarette sitting in a launderette
Hey Dad you're a drag — shopping bag.

Clean hair, comfy chair, you're really square
Being rude in the nude playing with your pubic cube.

What's your scene — daddio?
A real square dame — docido.
You're so uncool — eskimo.
Give me a dog — a bonio.
I'm the wild man — from Borneo.
My washing's done — it's time to blow.

der *Beat Poet*

BOTTOM LINE ■

An asshole is a part of man
Ever since the world began
A tasteless image it arouses
So it's hidden away, inside trousers.

White and pimply, lacking grace
It makes the world an ugly place
So for the end, the end has come
Join with me and ban the bum.

TH= TW·· R··N··
Problem Page

Dear Ron and Ron,

Many, many thanks for your advice and help. As you recall I was suffering from acute migraine, also I was trying to diet, rather unsuccessfully. But full marks to the Two Rons, you paid me a visit and now I'm completely cured. Since you sawed my hand off my migraine has completely disappeared, and my diet is going extremely well as I have not got a mouth to put any food in. Two Rons did make it right.

Yours thankfully, Eddie Boleyn.
P.S. Want to buy a hat?

Ron and Ron say,

We'd likc to say we're really glad you're a lot better, but we couldn't care less.

Dear Ron and Ron,

The other night I went to sleep, just like any other night, but when I woke up I found to my horror that my "thingy" had dropped off. Please, please help me.

Ron and Ron say,

Well, Mr John 'No Willy' Thompson, 11 Green Crescent, Birmingham, the answer to your problem is obvious. Your head is on back to front. To double check, see if you have grown a tail recently.

Dear Ron and Ron,

My wife and I enjoy what we consider to be a full and natural sex life, but our friends consider us strange and exhibitionist. For example, last Friday we threw a dinner party for a few close friends. We had seafood for starters and that always gets me and the wife going a bit so we thought nothing of shedding our clothes and having a right good session there and then in front of our guests on the table. Their embarrassment was heightened as we daubed each other's bodies with chunky cut orange marmalade and fresh yoghurt, and then licked it off, and then we set about spanking each other with a rolled up copy of *TV Times*. Tell me, are we in any way perverted?

Mr and Mrs Average, Nowheresville, Wilts.

The Rons say –

Of course you are! Everybody knows you should use ordinary orange marmalade. And by the way, when are you inviting us round for dinner?

Dear Ron and Ron,

I'm very worried about my 14 year old daughter. I've worked very hard to send her to the best schools in the country, but her behaviour is of grave concern to me. Not once have I heard her blow off. I've thought about taking her to a specialist, but you know how sensitive girls of that age are. Please help . . . .

Ron and Ron say,

Now this is a bit of a diffy. You're right, there seems to be a growing trend of young women who arc not willing to let rip in public, it's disappointing but it's true. Whatever happened to those halcyon days when your girlfriend would blast one out in a busy pub, and all that would be heard afterwards was polite admiring applause. That was when the miniskirt really came into its own.

The best thing to do to encourage your little girl is to use the catalogue of Post Fart Phrases. After you've dropped an audible trouser-cough, or pant-splitter, try one of the following phrases:

a) Speak up Brown, you're through.
b) More tea, vicar?
c) Get out and walk.
d) A pint of the usual.
e) Doctor!
f) Better out than in.
g) It's San Andrea's fault.
h) I've just farted.

See how you get on but don't worry too much, it will all come out in the wash!

FOOT FETISHISTS CALENDAR

Miss September

SCRATCH 'N' SNIFF

Miss September, a very popular lady . . . especially if you went to public school . . . A fragrance which says Nanny, Matron, red-raw bottom. A bouquet of barbed comment. The more mature perfume of blue stocking leaking into the ancient leather with more than a hint of wet dreams in the dorm. You'll scratch, sniff and scratch again.

COOKING CHEZ LES DEUX RONS

Foreword by
ROBERT CARRYOUT

"Cooking Chez Les Deux Rons" gives a unique insight into the world of gangland cuisine. All of the dishes developed by "Les Messieurs Rons" have their roots firmly planted in genuine East London recipes just as many former business associates of "Les Messieurs Rons" once had their roots firmly planted in Ron's girlfriend and now have them firmly planted in the Hammersmith Flyover.

The original ideas of "Cuisine avec un soupçon de Violence" were developed by Ron and Ron in their first restaurant. As Ron says:

"When we first opened up we named the restaurant after Ron's girlfriend Catherine. So we called it Ron's Caff".

With the help of their chef, Gordon Blue, the local rabbi, they continued to open up both restaurants and faces throughout the London area. As Ron says:

"In the early days we didn't have much dosh, so a knife would have to serve two purposes . . . know what I mean?"

Ron and Ron have been close friends of mine ever since they obtained the negatives of me with the donkey in Amsterdam. So it is without hesitation that I recommend their new cookery book to you. Their recipes are ideal for a dinner for four people . . . you don't like.

▶

COOKING CHEZ

DEVILLED KIDNEYS

We always like to go for the kind of meal that makes your tastebuds explode, or any other part of your body come to think of it. You could do a lot worse than try our Devilled Kidneys in Napalm Sauce, it doesn't cost too much so it won't leave a hole in your pocket, although it might leave a hole in your cheek.

1. First of all you need two kidneys. You can get these from your butcher, supermarket, or if you're very sneaky your local hospital.

2. Stick them in a whatchamacallit and liberally spice with ground glass, toenails and bird droppings. This will give you that lovely crunchy texture.

3. Cremate them in the oven for 10–15 minutes, or until they are thoroughly burnt. Serve with a dollop of brown sauce. (Remember when you take the whatchamacallit out of the oven don't use oven gloves – that'll bloody well teach you!)

To go with this we recommend a selection of vegetables. If the people who are coming to dinner are a pain in the arse, we recommend you give them the onions from the bottom of the vegetable rack. You know, those ones that look like a bunch of daffodils. To go with it what about

those carrots that are mouldering away beside them, those ones what have gone all sloshy and are wearing a fur coat? Don't forget those mouth-watering potatoes with that lovely wrinkly skin that has just gone to seed. Maybe you shouldn't have kept them under the stairs for the past year.

So get all your veg, peel them nice and slowly, you can almost hear them

LES DEUX RONS

scream. Then get a really sharp knife and slice 'em up, then boil them – alive – for quarter of an hour. If the potatoes get cheeky at all, give 'em a good poke with a fork, little tip for you, remember to leave their eyes in, it's a lot more painful. After boiling, smash 'em to bits, then slap it on a plate with the kidneys. Use your fingers if you haven't got a serving spoon, but only if you haven't been to the bog for the last couple of hours.

Now sit back and enjoy watching your guests slowly choke to death as you make a start on your fish and chips from round the corner.

DOCTORS WORDY

(Gareth as Doctor walks into Consultant's
(Norman's) Surgery.)

GARETH

Sir Arthur? Sir Arthur Ritus?

NORMAN

Lance, old boil, good of you to burst in. How the health are you? Fit?

GARETH

No thanks, just had one.

NORMAN

How long is it since you jaundice here?

GARETH

Well, I've been in the malaria for nine mumps now.

NORMAN

And how do you feel within yourself?

GARETH

Let me say without gout, your operation is eczmaceptional, and thanks very much for all your hospitality.

NORMAN

Well, I'm beri beri pleased to hear you say that. You have just been on holiday haven't you? Where did you go for the vaccination, Ulcer?

GARETH

No, actually I went to Sprain.

NORMAN

Oh — incontinent were you?

GARETH

For most of the time, yes. I went with Rubella, my girlfriend, and another couple, Ella and Sam, but Sam and Ella made me sick. I lint them some money, a measley sum I grant you, but I was rather whooping they'd cough up, and they didn't. Then, even worse, Sam went swimming with Rubella and had a stroke. I've never been so consulted in all my life, the pair of them were a pain in the botulism.

NORMAN

Yes, with friends like that who needs enemas? Relax Lance, don't get so hot under the cholera. You go thrushing around making rash decisions, now what will that hernia? Why don't you go and see a film or something, there's a good one on down at the Plasma, Herpes the Love Bug.

GARETH

Actually I caught that one last week. I think I'll go home and relapse, read a book by Nunion or that Ernest Haemorrhoid.

NORMAN

Ernest Haemorrhage — you bloody clot! Come and see me in a week, I'm pennicillin an appointment for you. I must be off, I've got a very strange case to deal with . . . a chap with a handkerchief growing out of the back of his neck.

GARETH

What do you think it is?

NORMAN

Legionnaire's Disease.

GARETH

Yes, I must rush off as well, there's something wrong with my girlfriend's foot.

NORMAN

Verrucca?

GARETH

I might do, mind your own business.

(EXIT)

PRIVATE NATIONAL HEALTH SERVICE
MEDICAL CARD
ISSUED BY THE
"Very Long Life" Insurance company.

please attach a £5-00 note to this card when you next visit your Doctor.

DATE OF BIRTH
1 1 61

Please quote this number if you write to the Family Practitioner
Number £5 00

Please notify the Family Practitioner of changes of name or address and return this card to them. Make sure you tell your doctor, too.

Mr., Mrs., Miss. Anne Thripy
Address 7 Severn Avenue Bucks. H.G.V.
Postcode

NB.
PLEASE ATTACH A SMALL FEE.

Dr:
Postcode

BORING PEOPLE

Are you sick and tired of being labelled uninteresting by your workmates? Are you forever referred to as 'a humourless bastard' by your so-called friends down the pub? Then why not follow these simple ideas to turn yourself into the funny person you always wanted to be.

WARNING Remember humour is a weapon, and in the hands of an expert can be devastating in any social situation. So go carefully.

Warm Up
A warm up is essential for all funny people. Nobody gets up in the morning and is instantly funny, although Bernard Manning does manage this when he forgets to wear his pyjamas. So step one:
PUTTING YOURSELF DOWN
Go to the bathroom mirror and look at yourself. If you are a genuinely boring person, there is a good chance that you are ugly too. So stand in front of the mirror, with your weight evenly distributed on the balls of your feet, and savagely rip the piss out of yourself. If you look closely you'll find plenty of scope. Maybe you have a large nose. Use this. It may come in very handy for a few penis jokes when your humourousness is more advanced. It may be that you are middle-aged, as most middle-aged people are usually very boring indeed. There's plenty of scope for humour in your ageing features, the brown teeth, the receding gums, or maybe you're really lucky in having a lazy eye. Take the piss out of all, or any, of these things. If you practise on yourself alone in the bathroom, then you will soon be able to put yourself down in public to the universal acclaim of your peers. For example:

Friend (sarcastically)	Hey, Peter — why have you never had a girlfriend?
Peter (you)	Because I'm a fat, ugly bastard with a lazy eye.

To British people this is not the reply of a boring person. This is the reply of an interesting person with a good sense of humour. Anyone who is the butt of his own jokes is likely to become very popular indeed. Being popular is a great way of gaining confidence, and confidence is what you need for stage two.

BELITTLING PEOPLE WITH WORDS

A man who belittles himself is always allowed to belittle others as long as he doesn't go too far, too soon. For example:

DUKE OF EDINBURGH	Hello Peter, how are you?
PETER (you)	Fine thanks, Phil. I hear your missus is a really good shag.

Many people would find you funny and interesting for making such a remark, but tread carefully early on in a new relationship. One way of going about this is to collect a piece of valuable information which has been volunteered by your subject earlier in your conversation. Store this information and throw it back in his face at any given opportunity. For example:

Early in the conversation:

PETER (you)	Excuse me, but you don't look very well.
NEW FRIEND	No, I'm . . . well, actually my mother died yesterday . . . .

Five minutes later in the conversation:

NEW FRIEND	Well, Peter, it's Christmas time again. You know I really hate Christmas shopping.
PETER (you)	Well, New Friend . . . you'll have one less present to buy than last year.

You cannot lose with this ploy. If your New Friend has a sense of humour he will laugh along with your witty jape. If he doesn't laugh, then he is the one with no sense of humour. Q.E.D.

Once you have gained a reputation for being 'a bit of a laugh' you can expand your operations.

THE DOUBLE MEANING

The British are lucky as a nation of jokers because our language is beautifully suited to double meaning or *double entendre* as the French would say (which is ironic since the French have no idea of *double entendre* or they would have realised years ago that De Gaulle's famous nose was, in fact, his penis).

Remember: every sentence in English has a rude connotation.

Pounce on this immediately. Here are some key words to watch out for.

Come – This word is the king of implied filth. No matter how innocently it is used by a friend, to you, as a funny person, it will always mean orgasm. This one works every time:

Dentist's Receptionist	Hello Peter . . . would you like to come through
Peter (you)	I don't know about the 'through'

As a funny person never let a sentence with the word 'come' in it (there's a joke to be had there — a sentence with come in it is a very messy sentence indeed!) pass you by without letting everybody know that *you* know it's rude.

Stiff — always means an erection

Wind — always means farting

A big one — a penis

A small one — a penis

Banana — a penis

Cucumber — a penis, often used by funny people in the context of nuns

Candle — see 'Cucumber'

Ball — a testicle. Most often used in 'having a ball' or 'The Policeman's Ball', with 'come'. Probably the bedrock of British humour.

These are a few of the more obvious terms. Even now you have thought of others. You are probably even beginning to make up your own. A good exercise is to look around the house for ordinary household objects that could possibly have a rude double meaning. A vacuum cleaner is a good start. Once you have a good store of rude double meanings in your head, then do not hesitate to use them. Employ them at every opportunity except when in the company of people who have studied at Oxford or Cambridge, who will not understand them.

THE PHYSICAL OR PRACTICAL JOKE
The physical or practical joke has both great dangers and great rewards. In the right hands the rewards are immediate. People laugh readily at physical jokes, most TV and film comedy is based on physical jokes. If you want a quick laugh, just fall over. It doesn't matter where. Try it in the office, or on a crowded platform as you wait for the 8.14 to Charing Cross.
Many people are tempted to play physical or practical jokes on other people. This can be dangerous. If the joke misfires you can end up looking bad. In your early stages, make sure that you are the butt of the jokes. For example:

My friend's dad never misses the opportunity, when opening a door, of smashing the door against his foot and pretending that the door hit his nose. Try to learn to play the William Tell overture by slapping yourself hard on your cheeks. The harder you hit yourself, the more your friends will laugh.
    You may be able to come up with your very own physical joke. Practise almost tripping over. When you have perfected it, try it out in the office. This has two big advantages as a joke. Firstly you get the laugh for nearly falling

and secondly it gives somebody else in your group the chance to chime in with 'Enjoy your trip'. Your humour score is doubled. You get the first laugh and force somebody else into using the corny follow up.

If you *must* play a practical joke on somebody else, then make sure that, if it works well, *you* take the credit but if it fails then it was nothing to do with you. Practical jokes misfiring are one of the basic weapons of farce and we want to be funny, not farcical, don't we?

THINGS TO AVOID

Wit	Don't bother with wit. Wit is something for intellectual people who are not funny. If you make yourself witty you will end up like Auberon Waugh — someone with a silly name and no friends at all.
Satire	Forget it. It's what witty people think of as funny. It isn't.
Telling jokes	Don't do it. The most boring people tell jokes. Even a parrot can tell a joke. Once someone has told a joke to a group of friends, everybody in that group feels duty bound to tell a joke of their own. After ten minutes everybody is bored silly and the standard of joke has declined so that nobody is laughing. Don't be tempted. Like Practical Jokes, telling a joke has as many pitfalls as rewards. Leave it to the experts.

The Story of

Big John

St. Peter's Square you could see him arrive
In a sedan chair carried up shoulder high
Just a sign of the cross and a nod of the head
He never ate much – just wine and bread
    Big John – Big John Paul.

He got a crazy ole hat and a baggy ole dress
But he's a real tough critter – I must confess
In Piccadilly Circus or Londonderry
He'd never hail a cab, he'd just hail Mary
    Big John – Big John Paul.

If you like the Pope buy a souvenir
There's posters and tee-shirts and all kinds of gear
You can even buy forgiveness in the form of a soap
Just wash away your sins with a Pope-on-a-rope
    Big John – Big John Paul.

SHOE FETISHISTS CALENDAR

Miss December

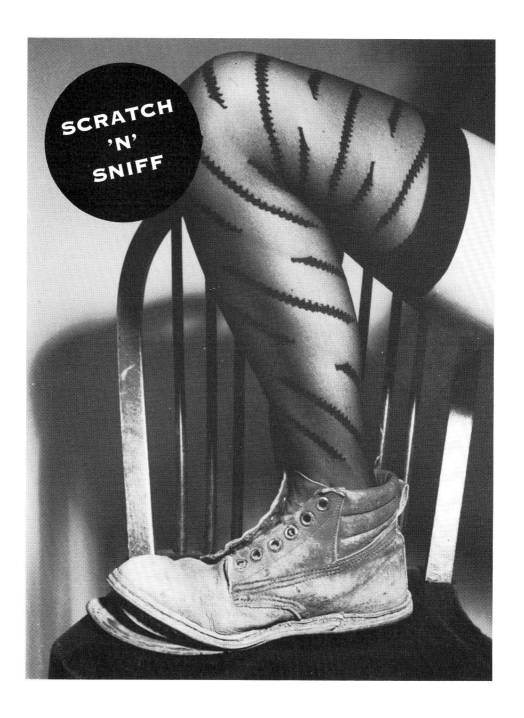

Ever fancied a bit of rough?? Well get your nose around Miss December. No
lady, this baby. An aroma which speaks of workman's sock and dead rodent.
Sniff this beauty for the double trouble effect . . . you can vomit and reach
orgasm at the same time . . . Happy inhalations.

CONFESSIONS
—— OF A ——
PIPE-SMOKER

I thought I was like all the other boys at school, but I wasn't. When my parents tucked me up at night I couldn't wait for them to leave the room, there was something I had to do. I waited and wanted all day long at school for that special moment and now in my darkened bedroom I was free at last, free to play with my pipe. Perhaps it was the touch of briar against my skin, maybe the slender lines of the stem, the bulge of the bowl, the heady aroma; I don't know but it was mine, all mine, that time of day I craved for.

As I got older I continued my secret sessions with my pipe, enjoying them more and more. My mother became suspicious eventually, she was aware I was at that certain age, and asked me if I had started having 'pipedreams'. She said it was nothing to be ashamed of, all young men went through this phase. I denied it strongly, but nonetheless I think she was unconvinced.

Things started to happen within my body, things I could not explain, my internal chemistry started to dictate a fresh need within me, I could not deny it. One day I started . . .

dressing up. Just my father's slippers at first, you know, the cherry red leather ones that click clack when you walk. I felt good, different somehow, complete. Before long it was the Arran cardigan, I liked the one with the buttons that looked like footballs. It was then that I noticed I had started talking to myself. The topics were always the same: gardening, car maintenance, and Do-it-yourself.

It was at this stage I started to seek the company of other pipe-smokers. I admit most of them were older men. I engineered meetings, I would deliberately walk down the road when Mr Jenkins, number 43, was washing his Marina. We would talk for ages about timing, tuning, fibre glass and the wonders of WD40. Then, one day, it happened, he asked me into his garage. It was like Aladdin's cave, a wonder of sprinklers, strimmers, wrenches, ladders and loft insulation.

From that day on I made my mind up, no matter what my parents thought, I would not be happy until I lived in a semi-detached house. No matter how much it hurt my parents I wanted to express myself as I really was, I wanted to be ordinary.

With Mr Jenkins, number 43's help I got a job, junior salesman for a reputable insurance company. My parents cried when I left home, even though I was only moving round the corner. I really enjoyed work, I could be myself.

I started for the first time to smoke my pipe in public. At first people turned and stared or muttered behind their hands, but I didn't care. Everybody in the office smoked a pipe, Alf, Wally, Nigel, even Mrs Scrivens the secretary.

Every third Friday in the month we would go for a half at our local, it was then I realised the joys of being a pipe smoker. Not only could I make my own clothes and hair stink, I could contaminate people within a twenty-five yard radius. Slowly my teeth were getting browner and were gradually eroding nicely where my stem had been resting on them all my waking day. As I blasted huge clouds of stinking, pipe smoke in that enclosed space I felt at one with myself. As I tapped out another bowlful of burnt-out baccy a hand touched my shoulder. I turned. It was Mr Jenkins, number 43, he persuaded me to fill up with a bowlful from his moist-maker pipe-master pouch. I drew hungrily on my pipe, the fumes were beautifully noxious, almost making me pass out. A man in the corner asked if someone had lit a bonfire and thrown a car tyre on it.

Mr Jenkins and I saw more of each other since that day in the pub. We are thinking of building a cloche together, for early veg. Things are rosy in the garden, in the garage and in the loft.

I'm not ashamed of what I am, there are many people like me, pipe-smokers with a penchant for a mobile home. And as long as insurance has to be sold, or there's a back garden to be dug over come November we'll be there. Someone's got to do it.

Do you want a face like Nancy Reagan's? Would you like to look like Joan Collins? If you would, then I'm not having you teaching rugby to my son any longer. But why pay through the nose for your nose job? Don't pay over the top for a slice off the bottom, don't part with quids for a new pair of dids. Now's your chance to do your own cosmetic surgery, on the cheap with our once in a 'slice-time' offer. Your very own Do-It-Yourself Cosmetic Surgery Kit. Including:

*1 Retractable knife
Ideal for hacking away that unwanted blubber. Whether it's that floppy bit of old git dangling under your chin, that egg-box patterned cellulite at the top of the thigh. Or if you fancy making that pair of diddy's you've always dreamed about, then just slit it open, fold back the old flesh, stick in the silicone and Bob's your aunty.

*1 large bulldog clip
Just tightly gather up all that spare old skin at the back of your neck and get a friend to place it between the jaws of the bulldog clip. Now look in the mirror. That ventriloquist's dummy's look at a fraction of the price Nancy, Joan and Zsa Zsa paid for it. And what's more, it's reversable. Just remove the clip, and you're back to your old self again. . . . And I do mean old.

*1 dead cat
Cut out the middle man — make your own cat-gut and use it with any old sewing needle at your own convenience.

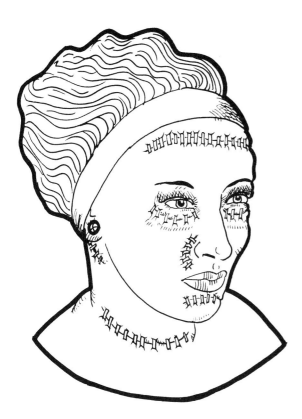

*Staple gun and staples
A must for closing up the wounds on the face leaving a nice 'punk jewellery' look for weeks afterwards.

GBH APPROVED

RABID ATTENBOROUGH

REPORTS FROM SOUTH AMERICA

I can hear the strange haunting pipe music of South America. South America, the land that has more piped music than a five-star hotel lift.

South America has recently become very fashionable, and at the moment it is very much the 'in' continent. But we are here today to uncover a place that has been a mystery since the very dawn of time. To do this we came by way of Titacaca, and we will be returning by way of Titibusbus.

I am at this very moment standing in Llamapoopoo, a breathtakingly primitive native village. A village that is solely populated by Amazon women and pygmy men.

Before me I can see a typical pygmy male. This type is quick, brown and foxy and is often seen jumping over lazy dogs. The Amazon women are tall and tanned and young and lovely, the girls from Llamapoopoo go walking . . . . sorry.

The women here are clad only in a flimsy loincloth, which makes it easy for them to run through the jungle, but it makes it very hard for the cameraman to keep his camera steady. As we hack our way into this clearing we can see a couple foraging for food. They work as a team, the female uses her height to reach fruit up in the trees, while the pygmy will often find his nuts on the ground.

They also combine their talents whilst hunting for game. The Amazon women are experts with a bow and arrow, made from the surrounding trees, and they have been known to make themselves a quiver occasionally. Yes, the art of Toxopholy, which is the way I always speak. As we meander through the village we can see pygmies making the deadly blow-pipes. These can be anything up to five feet long, and sometimes to blow is quite a job.

Today is the great Nuptial village ceremony, where the Amazon wives traditionally bathe their husbands in the river. And what a fantastic sight it is here at the riverside, watching the Amazon women washing their smalls in the basin.

LOCKETT 88

THE HIGHWAY CODE FOR LORRY DRIVERS

To drivers of lorries, especially Heavy Goods Vehicles.
Before driving _make sure that:_

1. **Pull out without warning when overtaking on a motorway.**

2. **Cut up all car drivers and cyclists on roundabouts.**

3. Your vehicle has *please wash me* inscribed in the dirt on the rear doors.

4. Drive through the parts of towns that are obviously far too narrow for your vehicle.

HAND SIGNALS

Narrow Tunnel Ahead.

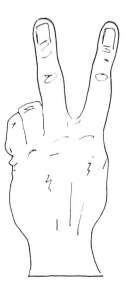

Two Way Traffic.

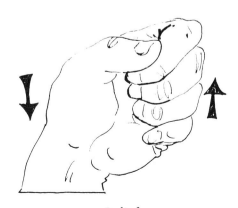

Relief Driver.

Average Speed
for HGVs.

Average IQ
for drivers.

Two sausages
and egg.

Bollocks. Who's
going to argue with a juggernaut.

Attach to your
underpants.

Articulated lorry driver.

Inarticulate lorry driver.

Wear a condom.

Max. Headroom

Straight On

Turn Left

Half past nine.

Spaghetti Junction

BILLY AND JOHNNY'S BEDTIME STORY . . .

Hello children — it's storytime

I wonder what the story is about tonight?

I wonder as well

Shall we have a look?

Shall we?

O.K.

Once upon a time Harry Hare was busy hopping through the woods. Hippety hop, hippety hop, hippety hop. He hopped so much he became very, veery tired.

Harry Hare sat down on a toadstool.

'Sorry Mr Toad,' said Harry.

'My pleasure,' said the toad.

Harry carried on. Hop leap bound, hop leap bound, hop leap bound. Oh look! He could see his old friend slowly coming towards him. It was Billy Burke the tortoise.

'Late again,' Harry cried.

'Sorry Harry, but I'm a silly billy, and I can only walk veery, veery slowly.'

Harry Hare said, 'Come on, Billy, these woods are getting dark, and besides what about the goblins?'

'Blow the goblins,' said Billy Burke. The two friends carried on and by now it was getting really dark.

They found themselves in a clearing. Billy Burke the tortoise had to stretch his head out of his shell to see, which made him look like Jack Palance.

Harry Hare started to burrow. His feet quickly dug into the soft earth.

'Give me a hand,' said Harry Hare.

Billy Burke helped him.

Soon they were dragging the freshly buried corpse from the grave.

Harry Hare said, 'The doctor will pay us handsomely for this one, it's still warm.'

Then they ran as fast as they could to the laboratory, which isn't very fast when you're a tortoise. The doctor gave them lots of cakes and sweets, they were so happy, Billy and Harry, those two cuddly bodysnatchers, Burke and Hare.

22nd Century Folk Song

On Monday I was walk-i-ng
Along the Old High Street
I heard a r-umb-ling in my tum
I knew I had to eat.
I saw a traditional English place
Where Englishmen are fed.
Inside the man with the hairy arms
To me he duly said

CHORUS
You want kebab? You want kebab?
Whack to me dear old flab
The shifty sod with the hairy arms
Said do you want kebab?

He smiled at me through his broken teeth
As he carved the half-cooked mince
Whilst covering the pocket of pitta bread
With his filthy fingerprints

He wiped his greasy fore-i-head
With his filthy greasy hand
Then he wrung the oil from his greasy hair
Into the old chip pan.

CHORUS
You want kebab? You want kebab?
Whack to me dear old flan
The greasy sod wrung his greasy hair
Into the old chip pan.

I took it and unwrapped i-it
And me eyes they opened wide
To see all the nourishing healthy things
That he had put inside
A lump of fatty gris-tle
Within that bread so stale
The ash of a Turkish cigarette
And a broken fingernail.

Dance break — breakdance.

So listen all you jolly boys
Who want a dainty dish
Then try a pile of donna
Or perhaps a pile of shish.

For just one bronzen pound coin boys
This bargain waits for you
You'll not just get a nourishing meal
But salmonella too.

CHORUS
You want kebab? You want kebab?
Rush to the nearest loo
You'll not just get a nourishing meal
But salmonella too.

TIME IS SHORT

Heed these words carefully, lest you should meet an untimely, agonising death.

*There is a land not far from here called Myrea. It is ruled over by Prong, King of the
Myreans, and all the people did pay homage unto their King saying,
'Oh, great Prong' and this made the King swell with pride.
But one of their number would not bend before the mighty Prong, and he was known
as the wizard, Borrix.
And the King did grab the wrinkled old Borrix, and did tie upon Borrix an heavy
load, and did banish the wizard from the land. And where'er he did walk people would
stop and look and say,
'Oh, so this is the load of Borrix I have heard so much about.'
And Borrix did put a spell upon the land so that it would be forever winter. So it
came to pass that Myrea and Prong were frozen stiff.
Now Prong did have two sons and they were called Koff and Kinnell, and both did
wish to rule over the Kingdom. And the King did say,
'It would hurt me deeply to divide Myrea, my sons. We will let the people decide.'
And the people did gather in the Square of the Hypoteneuse and the King asked them
to vote. Some did shout 'For Koff, for Koff, and those who did gather in the coldest parts
did cry 'Kinnell'.
So the King sent his sons away saying '. . . whosoever shall find the secret of warmth
shall lord it over Myrea for ever and a day.' Koff did journey to the land of many trees,
across the forest of mysteries, amid the branches of the Styx, and through the trunks of
the professional wrestler. But the wizard's servants did capture Koff, and he was
dragged off by the warlocks.
But Kinnell did return to his country with the secret of the great warmth, saying
'I have travelled the messy road in the land of Bogge, and I have squozen by the hand
Zit, King of the Yellowheads, and I have been to the highest of the high, Everest, and
there I did learn the secret of the great warmth. So, fellow people of Myrea, I have but
one question before the frozen finger be upon ye . . . Have you thought seriously about
double glazing?'*

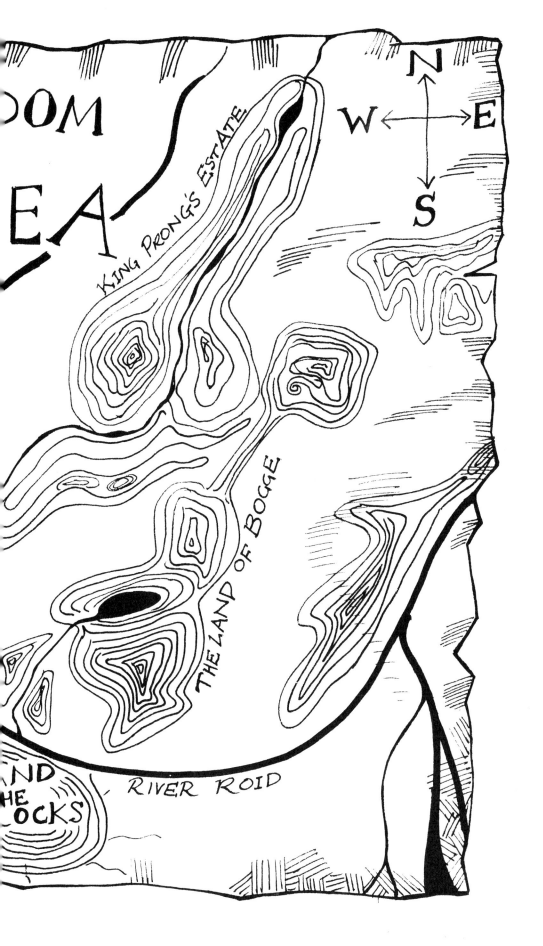

Handy Things for Xmas

BUY THIS FANTASTIC 'STREET-CRED' BRIEFCASE

■ No more of those leather 'I am a businessman' briefcases, this fantastic new concept in plastic is ideal for papers, files, sandwiches or shopping. Price £19.99 3721

REAL 22 CARAT GOLD INGOT 12″ × 4″ × 2″, weight 22 lbs.

■ Real 22-carat-gold ingot. This lump of real gold is an ideal paperweight. Stop those loose pieces of paper fluttering to the floor every time you open a door or window. Worth its weight in gold, it's a must! Price £4.99 3754

BOTTLE TOP ASHTRAY (actual size ¾ inch)

■ This terrific ashtray, taken off a beer bottle *by hand,* is ideal for the smoker who *doesn't* smoke that much. Also terrific and very, very ideal for the smoker who is trying to give up, and is too lazy to empty it. It's also terrific and marvellous and very ideal indeed for the smoker who doesn't smoke at all, the great thing is you don't have to empty it! Or why not use it for a bottle top? Price £15, pp. £22.50 3727

JAR OF FRESH AIR
■ Bring a breath of fresh air into your life with this 'Jar of fresh air'. This air is not like ordinary jars filled with air, our scientific experts have injected a special 'fresh' element. This could be a lifesaver if you are trapped in a submarine and really comes into its own if somebody next to you blows off. Send £10.99 now.   3763

IDEAL XMAS GIFT STORAGE HOLDER
■ This is the ideal container for all the fantastic presents your friends have bought you from this catalogue.   3963

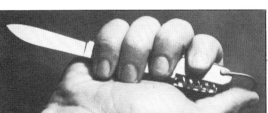

TREE AND
PENKNIFE SET
■ Ideal for the executive whose life is filled with stress, relax and whittle away your tree until all you're left with is a toothpick. Handy after business lunches. Price £11.99   3574

HANDY HIPPO
■ Be the envy of your friends, have a handy hippo in your living room. Ideal for getting rid of screaming brats.   3913

DOES YOUR *Husband* REALLY LOVE YOU?

Answer these questions to find out if yours is a marriage made in heaven. Add up the score and see how you did at the bottom of the page.

1 What is his pet name for you? Is it:
   a) Honey ☐
   b) Darling ☐
   c) Oy! ☐

2 When do you usually make love?
   a) At night ☐
   b) In the morning ☐
   c) When your husband is away ☐

3 When you are making love does he
   a) Whisper softly in your ear ☐
   b) Talk dirty ☐
   c) Fart and hold your head under the duvet ☐

4 What music arouses his passions?
   a) Ravel's Bolero ☐
   b) Frank Sinatra's greatest hits ☐
   c) Little Donkey ☐

5 On a romantic night out does he eat
   a) Chateaubriand ☐
   b) Lobster ☐
   c) Your edible knickers ☐

6 What would HE say if you caught him in bed with another woman?
   a) 'Sorry darling' ☐
   b) 'Let's talk this over' ☐
   c) 'Where did you hide my Johnnies?' ☐

7 Last Valentine's Day did he
   a) Take you for a meal ☐
   b) Take you to the pictures ☐
   c) Take the piss out of you in front of his mates ☐

8 For your anniversary did he give you
   a) Flowers ☐
   b) Lingerie ☐
   c) A pearl necklace ☐

9 If you had an industrial accident would he
   a) Carry you everywhere ☐
   b) Give up work to look after you ☐
   c) Get you a job in a circus ☐

10 Where did you first meet your husband?
   a) At work ☐
   b) Socially ☐
   c) In prison ☐

11 When your husband's ill, does he
   a) Lie in bed ☐
   b) Watch the TV ☐
   c) Try on your underwear ☐

12 Who does your husband most resemble?
   a) Paul Newman ☐
   b) Arnold Schwarzenegger ☐
   c) A bucket of sick ☐

SCORE
All a's You're a liar or you're lucky
All b's He's a creep or you're gullible
All c's You have understood the joke

Does He Love Me?

For Answers look to Page P37

HANDY HINTS FOR THE
Holocaust

LOCKETT 88

HANDY HINTS FOR THE HOLOCAUST

First things first

First of all – how do you recognise a nuclear attack?

Well, if you look out of your window and see a mushroom that's too big to fit into a frying pan you know you are in dead stook.

What do I do?
1) Cancel your milk and papers
2) Put the cat out
3) Turn off the gas, you don't want any nasty explosions
4) If you have got enough time fit a reputable draught excluder to all of your doors and windows.

HOW DO I BUILD A SHELTER?

Well most people go for the basement or under the stairs. Reinforce the walls with a bit of plywood, plasterboard or even a good thick anaglypta wallpaper. Maybe you're not one of those stay at home types. Maybe you are more of an outdoor type of person, like my mate Ralph, three doors down. He's got himself one of those new-fangled, lead-lined tents that comes complete with the free collapsible picnic table. Remember don't be afraid to experiment.

PROVISIONS

You are going to need provisions. Food, water and something to read. I recommend Teach Yourself Russian, because you never know who your neighbours are going to be. If you have got enough room, I find a recording of Al Martino's Spanish Eyes is particularly relaxing on those long radioactive evenings.

THE THREE MINUTE WARNING

This is a warning that is three minutes long. If you are peckish, I think you are talking soft boiled eggs. All you Mums out there, while Dad's doing the eggs, get your two-point-two offspring up to the smallest room for weewees and big jobs, and you still have time to give Cleo the goldfish a couple of pinches of food.

FALLOUT

This is a very nasty side effect, windows do it if you haven't used enough putty. It's called fallout because your hair, eyes, teeth and fingernails fall out, so remember to use that putty liberally.

WHAT NEXT?

Well, it's a case of sit and wait. Just pretend you're waiting for an interview at the DHSS. Remember it's not the end of the world, or is it?

THE SERGEANT MAJOR'S NATIVITY STORY

And it came to pass, in the land of Judaea, orders was posted that all squaddies should get fell-in for an roll call. And lo, Private Joseph Carpenter and his missus Mary was en route to report for duty at the barracks of Beff-le-Hem. Now then, Mary was nearing the end of her nine-month commission, and she was tired, she was fatigued, she was absolutely bleeding knackered. So Joseph, using his nous, being officer material, commandeered a donkey, Mary's bottom to sit on for the use of.

On arrival at Camp Beff-le-Hem, Joseph had a quick reconnoitre, only to discover that there was no bleedin' room at the inn, they was chock and block. Cock-up accommodation front!

Private Joseph, aware that Mary was only zero minus two hours from the big push, did use all available resources and did set up a bivouac in the stable around the Johnny Horner, and they did get dug in for the night.

During that night it was quiet. Perhaps too quiet. However, they pulled it off. The operation went like clockwork, the idea was brilliant, the conception was immaculate – not a speck of dirt to be seen anywhere. And there, lying in the manger, shining like a brightly polished button, was a little baby Jesus. And I tell you, that Mary weren't half chuffed.

And lo and be-bloody-hold, left right, left right, left right marching up to the stable comes the three wise men (probably from Intelligence) bearing gifts.

And it wasn't long before a platoon of shepherds turns up – beating an hasty retreat after a quick skirmish with an archangel. So picture the scene, on the right flank, wise men, on the left flank, shepherds, and forming the rearguard, donkeys, horses and sheepses.

Not many people know this but a young Sergeant Maji walked into Camp Beff-le-Hem that night, and he did look up and see a bright star shining up above a stable. And he did look up with wonderment and did say,

'Get that bleedin' light out!'

SOD OFF!